Wings of Wonder

"Exploring the Beauty, Diversity, and Conservation of Avian Life"

Cover Design by Shazia Naqib

To the Reader,

This book is dedicated to all those who find solace, inspiration, and wonder in the presence of birds. May their beauty and grace continue to uplift our spirits and remind us of the magic that surrounds us in the natural world.

With heartfelt gratitude,

Shazia Naqib

Contents

Introduction:
Welcome to the Mesmerizing World of Birds

Purpose of the Book
What to Expect

Chapter 1: The Diversity of Avian Life

Exploring the Incredible Variety of Bird Species
Diverse Habitats: From Tropical Rainforests to Arctic Tundras

Chapter 2: The Art of Birdwatching

Observing and Appreciating Birds in Their Natural Habitats
Birdwatching Equipment, Techniques, and Ethics

Chapter 3: Majestic Birds of Prey

Spotlight on Raptors: Eagles, Hawks, Falcons, and Owls
Hunting Behaviors, Nesting Habits, and Unique Adaptations

Chapter 4: Colorful Songbirds

Exploring the Vibrant World of Songbirds: Cardinals, Robins, Warblers, and More
Melodious Songs, Intricate Plumage, and Migratory Patterns

Chapter 5: Exotic Tropical Birds

Introduction to Stunning Tropical Birds: Parrots, Toucans,

Hummingbirds, and More
Brilliant Colors, Specialized Diets, and the Importance of Tropical Ecosystems

Chapter 6: Waterfowl Wonders

Dive into the World of Waterfowl: Ducks, Geese, Swans, and More
Migratory Journeys, Wetland Habitats, and Conservation Challenges

Chapter 7: Wonders of Flight

Fascinating Mechanics of Bird Flight
Evolution of Wings, Aerodynamics, and Marvel of Migration

Chapter 8: Threats and Conservation

Awareness About Threats Facing Bird Populations: Habitat Loss, Climate Change, Pollution
Highlighting Conservation Efforts and Success Stories

Chapter 9: Birds in Culture and Mythology

Significance of Birds in Human Culture, Art, and Mythology
Inspiration for Storytelling, Symbolism, and Spiritual Beliefs

Chapter 10: The Future of Avian Life

Importance of Protecting Bird Habitats and Biodiversity for Future Generations

Ways for Readers to Get Involved in Bird Conservation Efforts

Conclusion:
Reflecting on the Wonder and Beauty of Birds

Encouraging Readers to Continue Exploring and Protecting Avian Life

Appendix:

Glossary of Birding Terms
Recommended Resources for Further Reading
List of Birdwatching Organizations

A sneak paek into my next book

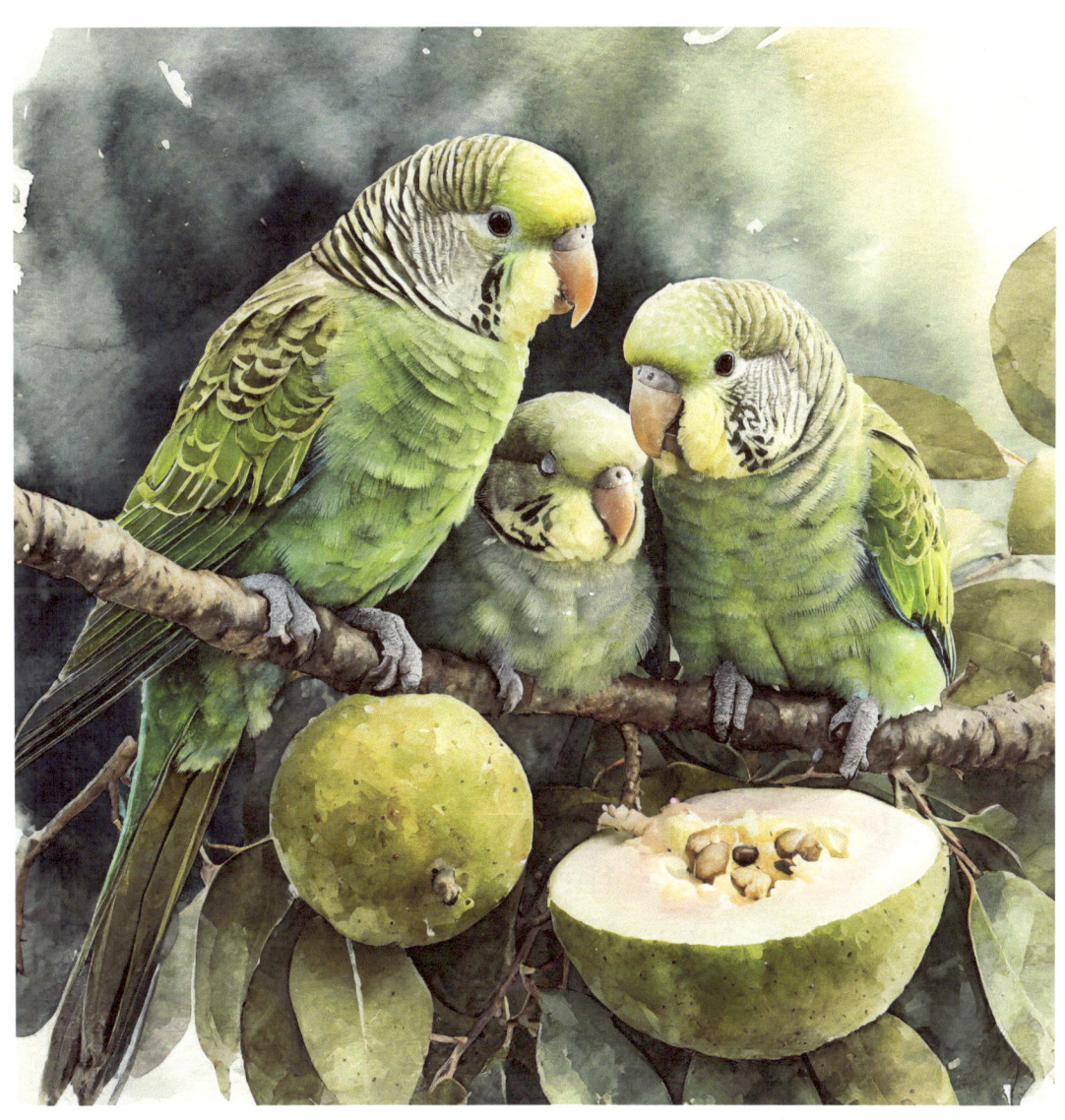

Wings of Wonder

Introduction: A Symphony in Flight

Welcome, dear reader, to the enchanting world of birds—a world where feathers are brushes painting the sky with hues of dawn and dusk, where songs are symphonies resonating through forests and fields, and where each beat of a wing is a testament to the enduring marvels of nature.

In the pages that follow, we embark on a journey that transcends continents and climates, exploring the diverse habitats that host some of the most wondrous creatures ever to grace the Earth: birds.

From the majestic eagles soaring over rugged mountain peaks to the tiny hummingbirds darting amidst tropical blooms, each bird is a masterpiece of evolution, adapted perfectly to its environment.

But this book is more than just a catalogue of avian species. It is an invitation to delve deeper into the lives of these feathered marvels, to witness their struggles and triumphs, to marvel at their beauty and complexity, and to contemplate our shared responsibility in ensuring their survival.

As we turn our gaze to the skies, we'll discover the art of birdwatching—an ancient pursuit that continues to inspire wonder and awe in those who partake. Through the lens of a pair of binoculars, we'll witness the intricate ballet of courtship displays, the fierce determination of a hunting predator, and the quiet moments of parental care in a hidden nest.

Throughout these pages, you'll encounter the regal raptors, the melodious songbirds, the exotic tropical species, and the graceful waterfowl that populate our planet. Each chapter is a celebration of the diversity of avian life, a testament to the ingenuity and resilience of these extraordinary creatures.

But our journey does not end with admiration alone. As stewards of this planet, we must also confront the challenges that threaten the survival of our avian companions. From habitat loss and pollution to climate change and poaching, the obstacles facing birds are daunting. Yet, there is hope in the tireless efforts of conservationists and the dedication of individuals around the world who strive to protect these fragile ecosystems.

So, dear reader, join me as we spread our wings and soar into the world of birds—a world of beauty, wonder, and endless discovery. Together, let us embark on an adventure that will inspire us to marvel at the magnificence of nature and to cherish the precious creatures that grace our skies.

For in the company of birds, we find not only solace and inspiration but also a profound reminder of our interconnectedness with all living beings on this fragile planet we call home.

Welcome to "Wings of Wonder: Exploring the World of Beautiful Birds."

Let the journey begin.

Chapter 1

The Diversity of Avian Life

In the vast tapestry of life on Earth, few groups of animals rival birds in their diversity and adaptability. From the icy realms of the Arctic to the steamy rainforests of the Amazon, birds have conquered almost every corner of the globe, evolving into a breathtaking array of shapes, sizes, colours, and behaviours.

Feathers: Nature's Masterpiece

At the heart of bird diversity lies a marvel of evolution: feathers. These intricate structures are not just for flight but serve a myriad of functions, from insulation and waterproofing to communication and camouflage. Feathers come in an astonishing array of shapes and colours, allowing birds to blend seamlessly into their surroundings or stand out in vibrant displays of plumage.

Adaptations for Survival

Each species of bird has evolved unique adaptations suited to its particular habitat and way of life. Consider the arctic-dwelling snow owl, with its thick downy feathers and keen hunting skills, perfectly suited to the harsh conditions of the tundra. Or the long-billed hummingbird, whose specialized beak allows it to extract nectar from deep within flowers, fuelling its frenetic flight.

Habitats Around the World

Birds can be found in virtually every habitat imaginable, from deserts and grasslands to mountains and coastlines. Some, like the penguins of Antarctica, are specially adapted to life in extreme environments, while others, such as the colourful parrots of the tropics, thrive amidst the lush foliage of rainforests. Each habitat presents its own challenges and opportunities, shaping the evolution of the birds that call it home.

Migration: A Global Phenomenon

One of the most remarkable feats of avian life is migration. Every year, millions of birds undertake epic journeys spanning thousands of miles, from breeding grounds in the north to wintering grounds in the south and back again. These migrations are driven by instinct, guided by celestial cues, and fuelled by an indomitable will to survive. From the iconic sandhill cranes of North America to the elegant swallows of Europe, migratory birds inspire awe and wonder as they traverse continents and cross oceans.

The Web of Life

Birds are not just isolated entities but integral parts of complex ecosystems, playing crucial roles in pollination, seed dispersal, pest control, and nutrient cycling. Their interactions with other organisms—whether as predators, prey, or competitors—help shape the balance of life in their respective habitats. As such, the conservation of birds is not just a matter of preserving individual species but safeguarding the intricate web of life that sustains us all.

Exploring Further

As we embark on our journey into the world of birds, let us marvel at the astonishing diversity of avian life and the myriad ways in which these remarkable creatures have adapted to the challenges of existence. From the icy peaks of the Himalayas to the steamy jungles of the Amazon, birds beckon us to explore, to discover, and to cherish the beauty of our natural world.

In the chapters that follow, we will delve deeper into the lives of birds, exploring their behaviours, habitats, and conservation challenges. But for now, let us pause to appreciate the sheer wonder of avian diversity and the boundless possibilities it holds for those who dare to look up and behold the skies.

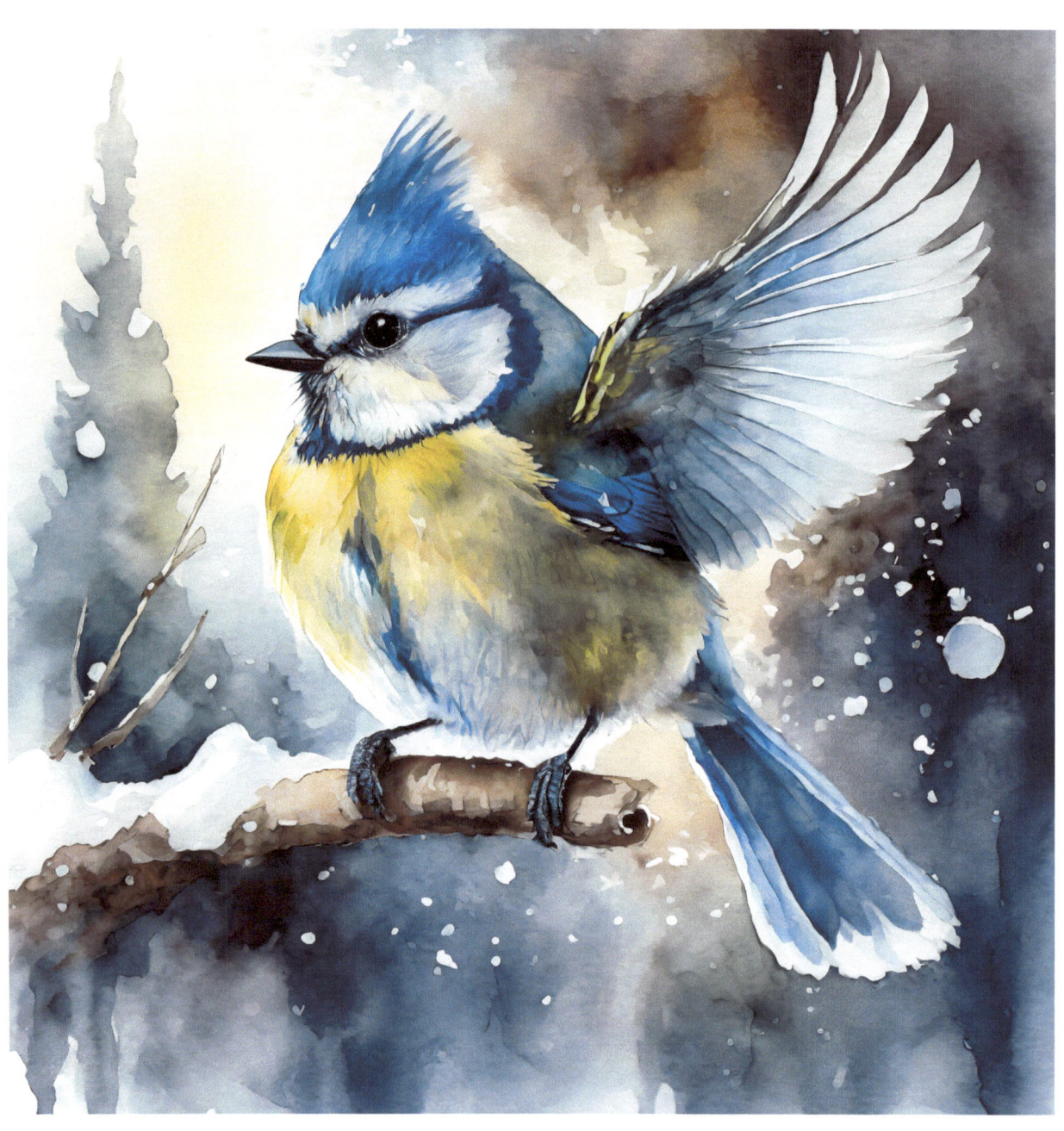

Chapter 2

The Art of Birdwatching

Birdwatching, or birding, is more than just a hobby—it's a lifelong pursuit fuelled by curiosity, patience, and a deep appreciation for the natural world. Whether you're a seasoned birder or a novice enthusiast, the joy of birdwatching lies in the thrill of discovery, the tranquillity of observation, and the sense of connection to something greater than us.

The Essentials of Birdwatching

To embark on a birding adventure, all you need are a few simple tools: a pair of binoculars, a field guide, and a keen eye for detail. Binoculars allow you to observe birds from a distance without disturbing them, while a good field guide helps you identify species based on their appearance, behaviour, and habitat. As you gain experience, you'll also learn to rely on your senses of hearing and intuition to locate birds hidden among the foliage.

Choosing the Right Spot

The key to successful birdwatching is finding the right habitat. Different species of birds prefer different types of environments, so it's essential to choose a location that matches your target species. Whether it's a woodland trail, a marshy wetland, or a coastal estuary, each habitat offers its own unique opportunities for birdwatching.

Patience and Persistence

Birdwatching requires patience and persistence. Birds are often elusive creatures and spotting them can sometimes feel like searching for a needle in a haystack. But with time and practice, you'll learn to recognize subtle clues—a flash of colour, a distinctive call—that lead you to your quarry. Remember, it's not just about ticking off species from a checklist but about immersing yourself in the sights and sounds of nature.

The Joys of Observation

One of the greatest pleasures of birdwatching is simply observing birds in their natural habitat. Whether it's the graceful flight of a heron, the intricate courtship dance of a grouse, or the playful antics of a flock of warblers, each encounter offers a glimpse into the lives of these fascinating creatures. Take the time to observe their behaviours, to marvel at their beauty, and to appreciate the intricate interconnectedness of life.

Ethical Considerations

As birdwatchers, it's important to prioritize the well-being of the birds we observe. Avoid disturbing nesting birds, refrain from playing recordings of bird calls to attract species, and always respect the natural habitats where birds live. Remember, our goal is not just to see birds but to ensure that they continue to thrive in the wild for generations to come.

Connecting with Other Birders

Birdwatching is not just a solitary pursuit—it's also a social activity that brings people together from all walks of life. Joining a local birding club or participating in organized birding events allows you to connect with fellow enthusiasts, share knowledge and experiences, and contribute to citizen science projects that help monitor bird populations.

The Endless Adventure

In the world of birdwatching, there's always something new to discover, always another species to add to your life list, always another mystery waiting to be unravelled. Whether you're exploring a familiar patch of woods or embarking on a birding expedition to a distant land, the adventure never ends. So grab your binoculars, open your field guide, and prepare to be amazed by the wonders of the avian world.

In the chapters that follow, we'll delve deeper into the lives of birds, exploring their habitats, behaviours, and conservation challenges. But for now, let us revel in the simple joy of watching birds in flight and the profound connection it brings to the natural world.

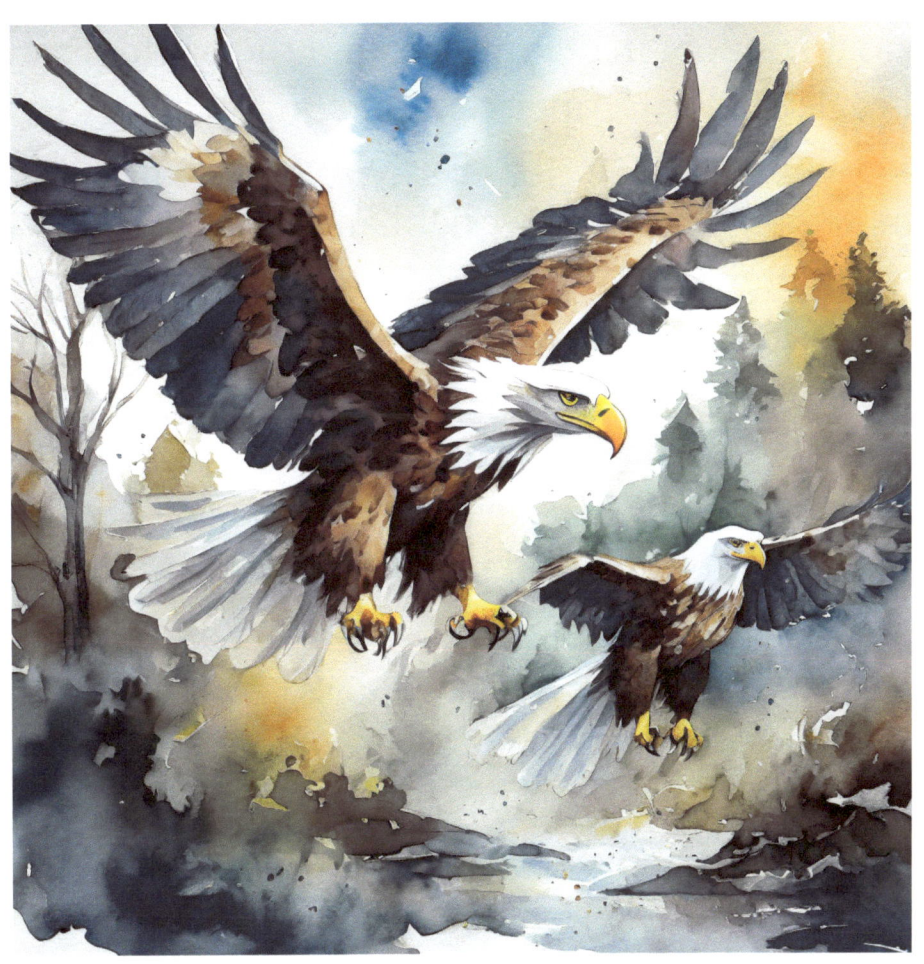

Chapter 3

TheMajestic Birds of Prey

In the realm of avian predators, few creatures command as much awe and respect as the majestic birds of prey. From the piercing gaze of an eagle soaring high above the mountains to the silent swoop of an owl hunting under the cover of darkness, these formidable hunters are masters of the skies, finely tuned by evolution for the pursuit of prey.

The Regal Eagles

At the top of the avian hierarchy stand the eagles, with their impressive wingspans and powerful talons. Found on every continent except Antarctica, these magnificent birds are symbols of strength and freedom in cultures around the world. From the iconic bald eagle of North America to the mighty harpy eagle of the Amazon rainforest, each species is uniquely adapted to its environment, employing keen eyesight and unmatched aerial prowess to hunt prey.

The Soaring Hawks

Hawks, with their broad wings and acute vision, are among the most agile and versatile of all birds of prey. From the swift peregrine falcon, capable of reaching speeds of over 240 miles per hour in a dive, to the stealthy red-tailed hawk, often seen perched atop roadside poles scanning for prey, hawks have adapted to a wide range of habitats and hunting strategies. Whether soaring high above open grasslands or weaving through dense forests, these graceful hunters are a testament to the power and grace of flight.

The Stealthy Owls

As creatures of the night, owls are shrouded in mystery and myth, their silent flight and piercing calls evoking a sense of otherworldly wonder. With their keen hearing and acute vision, owls are expert nocturnal hunters, able to pinpoint prey in complete darkness. From the great horned owl, with its distinctive tufts of feathers resembling horns, to the diminutive elf owl, the world's smallest owl species, these enigmatic birds play a vital role in controlling rodent populations and maintaining ecological balance in their habitats.

The Nimble Falcons

Falcons are the fastest birds in the world, capable of reaching speeds that rival those of fighter jets. With their sleek bodies and pointed wings, falcons are built for speed and agility, using their remarkable aerial acrobatics to chase down prey in mid-air. From the iconic gyrfalcon of the Arctic tundra to the elegant merlin of the temperate woodlands, falcons are consummate hunters, relying on a combination of speed, stealth, and precision to capture birds, insects, and small mammals in flight.

The Enduring Vultures

Despite their less-than-glamorous reputation as scavengers, vultures play a vital role in ecosystems by cleaning up carrion and preventing the spread of disease. With their keen sense of smell and impressive wingspans, vultures are often the first to arrive at a carcass, signalling to other scavengers that a feast is to be had. Despite facing threats from habitat loss, poisoning, and collisions with power lines, vultures are resilient creatures, adapting to changing landscapes and continuing to perform their essential ecological function.

Conservation Challenges and Success Stories

Despite their remarkable adaptations and ecological importance, birds of prey face numerous threats in the modern world. Habitat loss, persecution, pollution, and climate change are among the many challenges that endanger these magnificent creatures.

However, there is hope in the form of conservation efforts around the world. From reintroduction programs for endangered species to habitat restoration initiatives, dedicated individuals and organizations are working tirelessly to protect birds of prey and ensure their survival for future generations.

In the chapters that follow, we'll continue our exploration of the avian world, delving into the lives of colourful songbirds, exotic tropical birds, and graceful waterfowl. But for now, let us marvel at the majesty of birds of prey and the vital role they play in the intricate tapestry of life.

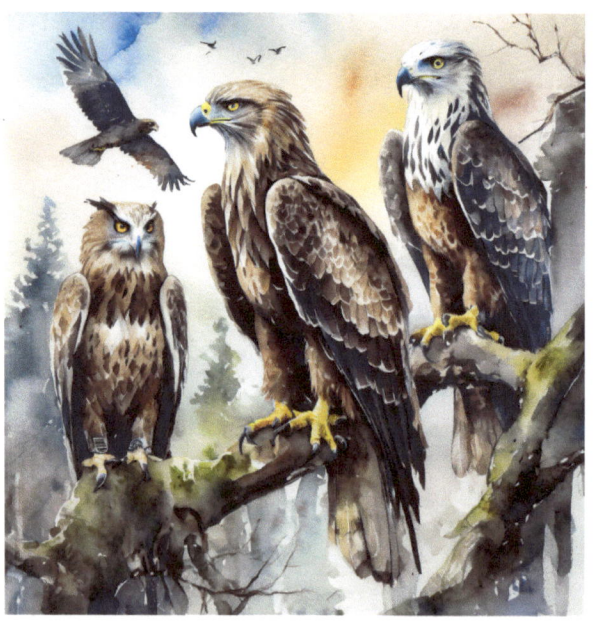

Chapter 4

Colourful Songbirds

In the world of avian beauty, few creatures rival the vibrant hues and melodious tunes of songbirds. From the dawn chorus of a spring morning to the gentle trill of a forest stream, these colourful creatures fill our lives with music and colour, enchanting us with their captivating songs and dazzling plumage.

The Symphony of Song

Songbirds, also known as passerines, are renowned for their complex vocalizations, which serve a variety of purposes, from attracting mates to defending territories. Each species has its own distinctive song, ranging from the melodic warbles of thrushes to the rhythmic chirps of sparrows. These songs are not just expressions of beauty but also vital forms of communication, allowing birds to coordinate breeding activities, warn of danger, and establish social hierarchies within their communities.

A Rainbow of Colors

In addition to their enchanting songs, songbirds captivate us with their brilliant colors and intricate patterns. From the fiery reds of cardinals and the electric blues of indigo buntings to the dazzling yellows of goldfinches and the iridescent greens of hummingbirds, each species boasts its own unique palette of hues. These vibrant colors are not just for show but also serve important functions, such as attracting mates, camouflaging against predators, and signaling social status within a group.

Migratory Marvels

Many songbirds are also renowned for their remarkable migratory journeys, undertaking epic voyages spanning thousands of miles between breeding and wintering grounds. From the iconic migrations of North American warblers, which travel from as far north as the Arctic Circle to Central and South America each year, to the transcontinental flights of European swallows, which journey from Europe to Africa and back again, these migratory marvels inspire awe and wonder in all who witness them.

Habitats and Adaptations

Songbirds inhabit a wide range of habitats, from dense forests and open grasslands to urban parks and suburban gardens. Each species is finely tuned to its particular environment, with adaptations ranging from specialized beaks for cracking seeds and probing for insects to nimble feet for perching and intricate nests for raising young. Despite their diverse lifestyles, songbirds share a common bond: a deep connection to the natural world and a reliance on healthy ecosystems for their survival.

Challenges and Conservation

Despite their beauty and cultural significance, songbirds face numerous threats in the modern world. Habitat loss, pollution, climate change, and predation by invasive species are among the many challenges that endanger these beloved creatures. However, there is hope in the form of conservation efforts around the world. From habitat restoration projects and breeding programs to public education initiatives and citizen science initiatives, dedicated individuals and organizations are working tirelessly to protect songbirds and ensure their survival for future generations.

In the chapters that follow, we'll continue our exploration of the avian world, delving into the lives of exotic tropical birds, graceful waterfowl, and fascinating birds in flight. But for now, let us revel in the beauty of songbirds and the joy they bring to our lives with their colourful plumage and enchanting melodies.

Introduction to Songbirds:

In the vast and diverse world of avian life, songbirds stand out as captivating marvels. Songbirds, scientifically known as passerines, belong to the order Passeriformes, encompassing over half of all bird species on Earth. What sets songbirds apart and makes them particularly captivating is their remarkable ability to produce melodious vocalizations, often accompanied by vibrant plumage and diverse behaviours. These avian virtuosos enchant us with their intricate songs, filling the air with melodies that evoke emotions and stir imaginations.

Diversity of Species and Habitats:

The diversity of songbirds is astounding, with thousands of species inhabiting a wide range of habitats across every continent except Antarctica. From the dense rainforests of the Amazon to the expansive grasslands of the African savanna, songbirds have adapted to thrive in diverse environments. Each species has its own unique set of characteristics, behaviours, and vocalizations, reflecting its evolutionary history and ecological niche.

In terms of species diversity, songbirds include an extensive array of families, such as thrushes, warblers, finches, sparrows, robins, jays, and wrens, among many others. Each family comprises numerous genera and species, exhibiting a stunning variety of

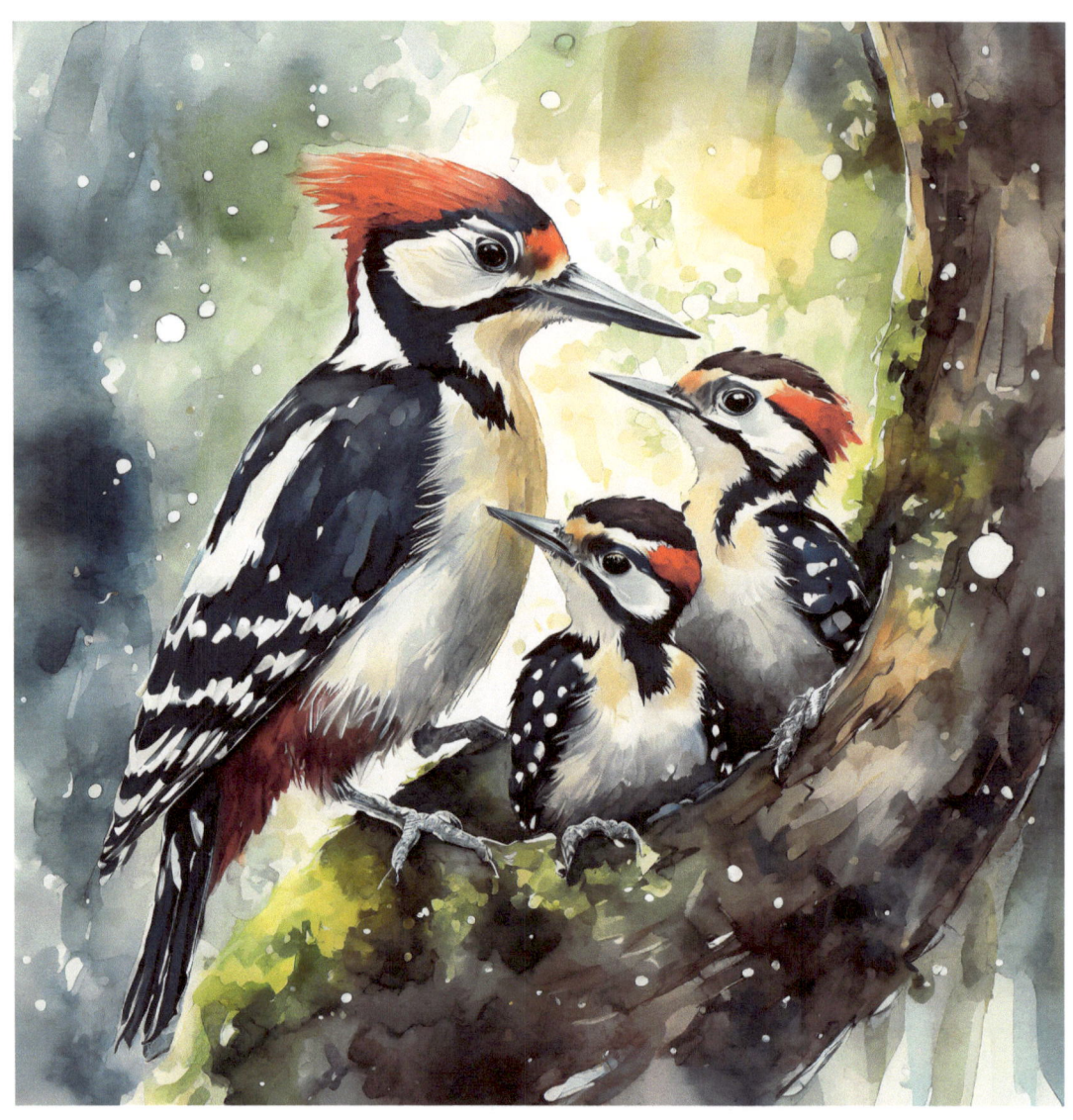

sizes, shapes, colours, and vocalizations. Whether it's the melodious trills of warblers echoing through the canopy or the cheerful chirps of sparrows in urban parks, songbirds offer an endless symphony of sounds and sights to explore.

Similarly, songbirds occupy an impressive range of habitats, from remote wilderness areas to urban environments and everything in between. Some species prefer dense forests, where they forage for insects and fruits amidst the canopy, while others thrive in open grasslands, where they build nests in low shrubs and grasses.

In Wetlands, deserts, mountains, and even suburban gardens are all home to a diverse array of songbird species, each adapted to its specific habitat requirements.

The adaptability of songbirds allows them to exploit a wide range of resources and niches within their habitats, making them integral components of ecosystems worldwide. Whether they are pollinating flowers, dispersing seeds, controlling insect populations, or serving as prey for predators, songbirds play vital roles in maintaining the balance and biodiversity of their respective habitats.

In the chapters that follow, we will delve deeper into the enchanting world of songbirds, exploring their melodious songs, vibrant plumage, fascinating behaviours, and the conservation challenges they face. Through our journey, we will gain a deeper appreciation for these captivating creatures and the rich tapestry of life they contribute to on our planet.

Physical Characteristics of Songbirds:

Songbirds, or passerines, are distinguished by several physical characteristics that contribute to their charm and allure. These features include their melodious vocalizations, vibrant plumage, and diverse feeding habits, each of which reflects the unique adaptations of these avian wonders.

Melodious Vocalizations:

One of the most defining characteristics of songbirds is their ability to produce complex and melodious vocalizations. Equipped with specialized vocal organs called syrinxes, songbirds have evolved a remarkable diversity of songs and calls used for communication, mate attraction, territorial defense, and social bonding.

The songs of songbirds vary widely in complexity, ranging from simple chirps and whistles to elaborate melodies consisting of multiple notes and phrases. Some species, such as thrushes and warblers, are renowned for their rich and melodious songs that fill the air with music, while others, like sparrows and finches, produce simpler but no less charming vocalizations.

Vibrant Plumage:

In addition to their enchanting songs, songbirds captivate us with their vibrant plumage, which comes in an astonishing array of colors, patterns, and textures. From the fiery reds and oranges of cardinals to the electric blues and greens of hummingbirds, songbirds are adorned in hues that rival the most dazzling of rainbows.

The bright colours of songbirds serve multiple functions, including mate attraction, camouflage, and species recognition. Males often exhibit more vibrant plumage than females, using their colourful feathers to attract mates during courtship displays. In some species, plumage colours also play a role in establishing dominance within the flock or signalling social status.

Diverse Feeding Habits:

Songbirds have diverse feeding habits, reflecting their adaptability to a wide range of environments and dietary resources. Some species, such as finches and sparrows, have stout, conical beaks adapted for cracking seeds and nuts, while others, like warblers and flycatchers, have slender, pointed beaks for catching insects in mid-air.

In addition to seeds and insects, songbirds may also feed on fruits, nectar, and even small vertebrates, depending on their dietary preferences and ecological niche. This diversity of feeding habits allows songbirds to exploit a wide range of resources within their habitats, contributing to their success and abundance in various ecosystems.

Overall, the physical characteristics of songbirds, including their melodious vocalizations, vibrant plumage, and diverse feeding habits, reflect the remarkable adaptations that have allowed these avian wonders to thrive and enchant us with their beauty and charm.

Role of Songs in Courtship and Mate Selection:

For songbirds, vocalizations play a pivotal role in courtship rituals and mate selection. Males use their songs to attract females and establish territories, demonstrating their fitness, genetic quality, and ability to provide for potential offspring. During the breeding season, males sing from prominent perches, proclaiming their presence and defending their territories from rival males.
The complexity and quality of a male's song are important factors in attracting a mate. Females often prefer males with more elaborate and consistent songs, as these qualities may indicate good genes, strong immune systems, and the ability to provide adequate parental care. Males invest considerable time and energy in perfecting their songs, with some species engaging in elaborate courtship displays that showcase their vocal talents and physical

prowess.

In addition to attracting mates, songs also serve as a form of communication between mated pairs, reinforcing pair bonds and coordinating breeding activities. Duets between male and female partners are common in some species, allowing them to synchronize their movements and defend their territory together. Overall, the role of songs in courtship and mate selection among songbirds highlights the importance of vocalizations in reproductive success and species survival.

Migration Patterns:

Many songbirds undertake remarkable migratory journeys each year, traveling thousands of miles between their breeding and wintering grounds. These migrations are driven by seasonal changes in temperature and food availability, prompting birds to seek more favourable conditions elsewhere. Migration is a perilous undertaking fraught with challenges, including exhaustion, predation, adverse weather conditions, and habitat loss.

During migration, songbirds rely on a network of stopover sites to rest and refuel along their journey. These stopover sites, which include coastal areas, wetlands, and forested habitats, provide crucial resources such as food, water, and shelter, allowing birds to replenish their energy reserves before continuing their journey. The availability and quality of stopover sites are critical factors in determining the success of migratory journeys and the survival of songbird populations.

In recent years, climate change and habitat destruction have posed additional threats to migratory songbirds, altering the timing and distribution of food resources, and disrupting traditional migration routes. Conservation efforts aimed at protecting stopover sites and preserving critical habitats are essential for ensuring the survival of migratory songbird populations in an increasingly challenging and uncertain world. Through coordinated international cooperation and habitat restoration initiatives, we can work together to safeguard the long-term viability of these fascinating avian travellers and the ecosystems they depend on.

Migration of Songbirds:

Each year, millions of songbirds embark on remarkable migratory journeys spanning thousands of miles between their breeding and wintering grounds. These migrations are among the most fascinating phenomena in the natural world, as songbirds navigate vast distances with remarkable precision and endurance. The migration of songbirds is driven by seasonal changes in temperature, food availability, and daylight hours, prompting birds to seek more favourable conditions elsewhere.

Challenges During Migration:

Migration is a perilous undertaking fraught with numerous challenges that songbirds must overcome to successfully reach their destinations. One of the greatest challenges is the physical exertion required for sustained flight over long distances. Songbirds often fly non-stop for hours or even days at a time, covering hundreds of miles without rest. This constant exertion places considerable strain on their bodies, requiring them to consume large amounts of energy to fuel their flight.

Through coordinated international cooperation, habitat restoration initiatives, and public education efforts, we can work together to safeguard the stopover sites that are vital for the survival of migratory songbirds. By protecting these critical habitats and addressing the threats they face, we can ensure that songbirds continue to enchant us with their migratory journeys for generations to come.

Iconic and Colourful Songbird Species:

1.	Scarlet Tanager (Piranga olivacea):

•	Natural History: The Scarlet Tanager is a striking songbird found in the forests of North and South America. Males are vibrant scarlet red with black wings and tail, while females are olive-green with yellowish underparts. They primarily feed on insects, fruits, and berries.
•	Distribution: Scarlet Tanagers breed in deciduous and mixed forests across eastern North America and migrate to northern South America for the winter.
•	Conservation Status: While Scarlet Tanagers are not currently considered globally threatened, they face habitat loss and fragmentation due to deforestation and urbanization in their breeding and wintering ranges. Conservation efforts focus on protecting intact forests and creating connectivity corridors to support their migration.

2.	Gouldian Finch (Erythrura gouldiae):

•	Natural History: The Gouldian Finch, also known as the Rainbow Finch, is native to northern Australia. Males display vibrant plumage with a mix of red, yellow, green, and blue, while females are more subdued in coloration. They primarily feed on grass seeds and insects.

- Distribution: Gouldian Finches inhabit open woodlands, grasslands, and savannas across northern Australia, particularly in the Kimberley region of Western Australia.
- Conservation Status: The Gouldian Finch is listed as Near Threatened due to habitat destruction, wildfires, and predation by invasive species such as cats and foxes. Conservation efforts include habitat restoration, captive breeding programs, and community engagement to raise awareness about the species' plight.

1. Golden Pheasant (Chrysolophus pictus):

- Natural History: The Golden Pheasant is a dazzling bird native to the mountainous forests of western China. Males are adorned with bright golden-yellow plumage, a scarlet crest, and ornate tail feathers, while females are more subdued with mottled brown and gray plumage.
- Distribution: Golden Pheasants inhabit dense forests and shrublands in central and western China, with introduced populations established in the United Kingdom and other parts of Europe.
- Conservation Status: Although not globally threatened, Golden Pheasants face habitat loss and degradation due to deforestation, agriculture, and human disturbance. Conservation efforts focus on protecting remaining forest habitats and regulating hunting to ensure sustainable populations.

4. Paradise Tanager (Tangara chilensis):

- Natural History: The Paradise Tanager is a dazzling bird found in the tropical forests of South America. Males exhibit brilliant turquoise-blue plumage with a green back and a red throat, while females are olive-green with yellow underparts. They feed on a diet of fruits, insects, and nectar.
- Distribution: Paradise Tanagers are distributed across the Amazon Basin, the Andes Mountains, and the Guiana Highlands in South America, where they inhabit humid forests and forest edges.
- Conservation Status: While Paradise Tanagers are not globally threatened, they face habitat loss and degradation due to deforestation, logging, and agriculture. Conservation efforts focus on protecting key habitats and implementing sustainable land-use practices to minimize human impacts on their ecosystems.

These iconic and colourful songbird species represent just a few examples of the remarkable diversity of avian life around the world. While each species faces its own conservation challenges, concerted efforts to protect their habitats and address threats can help ensure their survival for future generations to enjoy.

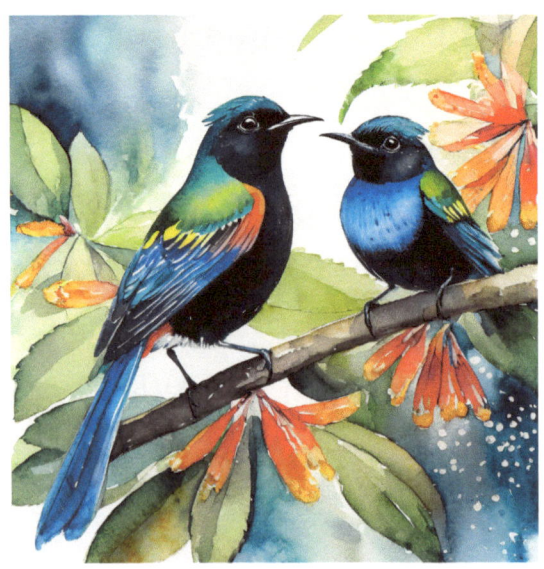

Chapter 5

Exotic Tropical Birds

Introduction:

Welcome to the vibrant and captivating world of exotic tropical birds, where dazzling colors, intricate plumage, and enchanting melodies converge to create a symphony of beauty and wonder. In this chapter, we embark on a journey into the lush rainforests, verdant jungles, and tropical paradises of the world, where a stunning array of avian treasures awaits discovery. From the flamboyant parrots and majestic toucans to the diminutive hummingbirds, tropical birds epitomize the splendor and diversity of tropical ecosystems, showcasing nature's boundless creativity and ingenuity.

Parrots:

Parrots, with their vibrant plumage, intelligent eyes, and charismatic personalities, are among the most iconic and beloved of all tropical birds. Found primarily in tropical and subtropical regions around the world, parrots exhibit a remarkable diversity of colors, sizes, and behaviors. From the brilliant blue-and-gold macaws of South America to the rainbow-hued lorikeets of Australia, parrots captivate us with their beauty and charm.

Toucans:

Toucans, with their oversized bills, vivid plumage, and distinctive calls, are synonymous with the tropical rainforests of Central and South America. These iconic birds play crucial roles as seed dispersers and pollinators in their ecosystems, using their long, serrated bills to reach fruits and flowers high in the canopy. From the iconic Keel-billed Toucan with its rainbow-colored bill to the striking Toco Toucan with its oversized orange beak, toucans are emblematic of the exotic allure of tropical forests.

Hummingbirds:

Hummingbirds, with their iridescent plumage, rapid wingbeats, and delicate beauty, are among the smallest and most enchanting of all tropical birds. Found exclusively in the Americas, hummingbirds are renowned for their hovering flight, long bills adapted for probing flowers, and extraordinary metabolism that enables them to sustain high-energy lifestyles. From the jeweled colors of the Ruby-throated Hummingbird to the dazzling displays of the Sword-billed Hummingbird, these tiny avian gems captivate us with their grace and agility.

Brilliant Colors and Specialized Diets:

One of the most striking features of tropical birds is their brilliant colors and intricate plumage, which serve a variety of purposes ranging from mate attraction to camouflage and species recognition. Many tropical birds, including parrots, toucans, and hummingbirds, exhibit vibrant hues of red, orange, yellow, blue, and green, often accentuated by iridescent or metallic sheens.

In addition to their stunning colors, tropical birds have specialized diets adapted to their unique habitats and lifestyles. Parrots, for example, are primarily frugivorous, feeding on fruits, seeds, and nuts, while toucans have a more varied diet that includes fruits, insects, and small vertebrates. Hummingbirds are nectarivores, feeding on the sweet nectar of flowers and supplementing their diet with insects for protein.

Importance of Tropical Ecosystems:

Tropical birds play integral roles in the health and functioning of tropical ecosystems, serving as pollinators, seed dispersers, and indicators of environmental quality. Their interactions with plants help maintain biodiversity, support ecosystem services such as carbon sequestration and water purification, and contribute to the resilience of tropical forests in the face of environmental change.

Tropical ecosystems, in turn, provide essential habitat for a vast array of plant and animal species, including many endemic and endangered species. These ecosystems are also vital for human well-being, providing valuable resources such as food, medicine, and clean water, as well as cultural and recreational opportunities for local communities and visitors alike.

Conclusion:

As we conclude our exploration of exotic tropical birds, let us marvel at the beauty, diversity, and importance of these remarkable creatures and the ecosystems they inhabit. From the vivid colors of parrots and toucans to the delicate grace of hummingbirds, tropical birds inspire us with their splendor and remind us of the extraordinary wonders of the natural world. By protecting tropical ecosystems and the biodiversity they support, we can ensure that future generations continue to experience the enchantment of tropical birds and the ecosystems they call home.

Chapter 6

Enchanting Waterfowls

Introduction:

In the tranquil realms of wetlands, lakes, rivers, and coastal estuaries, waterfowl reign supreme, captivating our hearts with their grace, beauty, and adaptability. From the elegant swans gliding serenely across mirrored waters to the raucous gatherings of ducks and geese in marshy habitats, waterfowl embody the essence of aquatic splendor. In this chapter, we embark on a journey into the enchanting world of waterfowl, exploring their diverse species, habitats, behaviors, and conservation challenges.

The Majesty of Swans:

Swans, with their long necks, graceful movements, and majestic presence, hold a special place in the hearts of many. Among the most iconic of all waterfowl, swans are renowned for their beauty, elegance, and symbolism. From the regal Mute Swan, with its pure white plumage and orange bill, to the bewitching Black Swan, with its sleek black feathers and vibrant red eyes, swans evoke a sense of awe and wonder wherever they roam.

Dabbling Ducks and Diving Ducks:

Ducks, with their distinctive quacks, colorful plumage, and endearing behaviors, are among the most familiar and beloved of all waterfowl. Dabbling ducks, such as Mallards and Northern Pintails, feed by tipping their bodies forward in shallow water to reach aquatic vegetation and invertebrates. Diving ducks, such as Canvasbacks and Redheads, are equipped with specialized adaptations for diving underwater in search of food, including streamlined bodies and webbed feet.

Gregarious Geese and Gaggles:

Geese, with their honking calls and V-shaped flight formations, are emblematic of wild spaces and open skies. Known for their strong family bonds and communal behaviors, geese gather in large flocks during migration and breeding seasons, forming impressive aerial spectacles as they traverse vast distances across continents. From the iconic Canada Goose to the diminutive Lesser Snow Goose, geese are a symbol of resilience, adaptability, and cooperation in the face of adversity.

Wetland Wonders and Coastal Charms:

Waterfowl inhabit a wide range of habitats, from freshwater marshes and swamps to coastal estuaries and open seas. Wetlands, in particular, are vital ecosystems for waterfowl, providing essential breeding, feeding, and resting grounds for millions of birds worldwide. Coastal habitats, including mudflats, salt marshes, and rocky shorelines, support a diverse array of waterfowl species, from shorebirds and waders to seabirds and sea ducks.

Conservation Challenges and Solutions:

Despite their resilience and adaptability, waterfowl face numerous conservation challenges in the modern world. Habitat loss, pollution, climate change, and hunting pressure threaten waterfowl populations and their habitats, endangering the delicate balance of aquatic ecosystems. Conservation efforts aimed at protecting wetlands, restoring degraded habitats, regulating hunting practices, and mitigating human impacts are essential for ensuring the survival of waterfowl for future generations to enjoy.

Birdwatching Adventures and Ecotourism Opportunities:

For birdwatchers and nature enthusiasts, waterfowl offer endless opportunities for exploration, discovery, and appreciation. From guided birding tours and wildlife cruises to remote birding hotspots and designated bird sanctuaries, there are countless ways to experience the wonder of waterfowl in their natural habitats. Whether observing courtship displays, witnessing migratory spectacles, or simply enjoying the tranquility of wetland vistas, waterfowl inspire us to cherish and protect the precious treasures of our natural world.

Conclusion:

As we conclude our journey into the enchanting world of waterfowl, let us reflect on the profound beauty, diversity, and significance of these magnificent birds. From the serene elegance of swans to the lively antics of ducks and geese, waterfowl embody the timeless allure of aquatic life, reminding us of the interconnectedness of all living things and the importance of preserving our planet's precious ecosystems. Through stewardship, conservation, and appreciation, we can ensure that waterfowl continue to grace our skies and waters with their presence for generations to come.

Chapter 7

Wonders of Flight

Exploring the Fascinating Mechanics of Bird Flight:

Birds, with their graceful aerial maneuvers and effortless soaring, are the masters of the skies, captivating us with their ability to defy gravity and navigate vast distances with precision and grace. In this chapter, we delve into the fascinating mechanics of bird flight, exploring the evolutionary adaptations, aerodynamic principles, and remarkable behaviors that enable birds to take to the air and conquer the heavens.

Evolution of Wings:

The evolution of wings is one of nature's most remarkable achievements, representing millions of years of adaptation and refinement. The earliest ancestors of birds were small, bipedal dinosaurs that gradually evolved feathers for insulation and display purposes. Over time, these primitive feathers became modified into specialized structures capable of generating lift and thrust, ultimately giving rise to the wings we see in modern birds.

Wings vary widely in shape, size, and structure among different bird species, reflecting adaptations to their specific lifestyles and habitats. Some birds, such as albatrosses and eagles, have long, narrow wings adapted for soaring and gliding, while others, like hummingbirds and kingfishers, have short, broad wings designed for agile maneuvering and hovering.

Aerodynamics of Bird Flight:

The aerodynamics of bird flight are governed by the principles of lift, drag, thrust, and weight, which interact to produce the forces necessary for sustained flight. Lift is generated by the shape of the wing and the flow of air over its surface, while drag is caused by air resistance and friction. Thrust is provided by the bird's wingbeats, which propel it forward through the air, while weight is countered by the lift generated by the wings.

Birds employ a variety of flight techniques to optimize their efficiency and performance in different environments. Gliding, soaring, flapping, and hovering are among the most common flight modes used by birds, each adapted to their specific needs and behaviors. Gliders, such as vultures and pelicans, use thermal air currents to stay aloft with minimal effort, while flappers, like hummingbirds and swallows, rely on rapid wingbeats to generate lift and thrust.

The Marvel of Migration:

Migration is one of the most awe-inspiring phenomena in the natural world, as birds undertake epic journeys spanning thousands of miles between their breeding and wintering grounds. Migration is driven by seasonal changes in temperature, food availability, and daylight hours, prompting birds to seek more favorable conditions elsewhere. Migratory birds use a combination of celestial cues, geomagnetic fields, and innate instincts to navigate with astonishing accuracy across vast distances.

Migration presents numerous challenges for birds, including fatigue, predation, adverse weather conditions, and habitat loss.

Stopover sites along migration routes provide crucial rest and refueling opportunities, allowing birds to replenish their energy reserves before continuing their journey. The success of migration depends on the availability and quality of these stopover sites, making their conservation essential for the survival of migratory bird populations.

Conclusion:

As we conclude our exploration of the wonders of flight, let us marvel at the ingenuity, adaptability, and resilience of birds in mastering the skies. From the evolution of wings and the principles of aerodynamics to the marvel of migration and the mysteries of navigation, bird flight is a testament to the beauty and complexity of the natural world. By studying and appreciating the mechanics of bird flight, we gain a deeper understanding of the extraordinary capabilities of these avian wonders and the importance of protecting their habitats and ecosystems for generations to come.

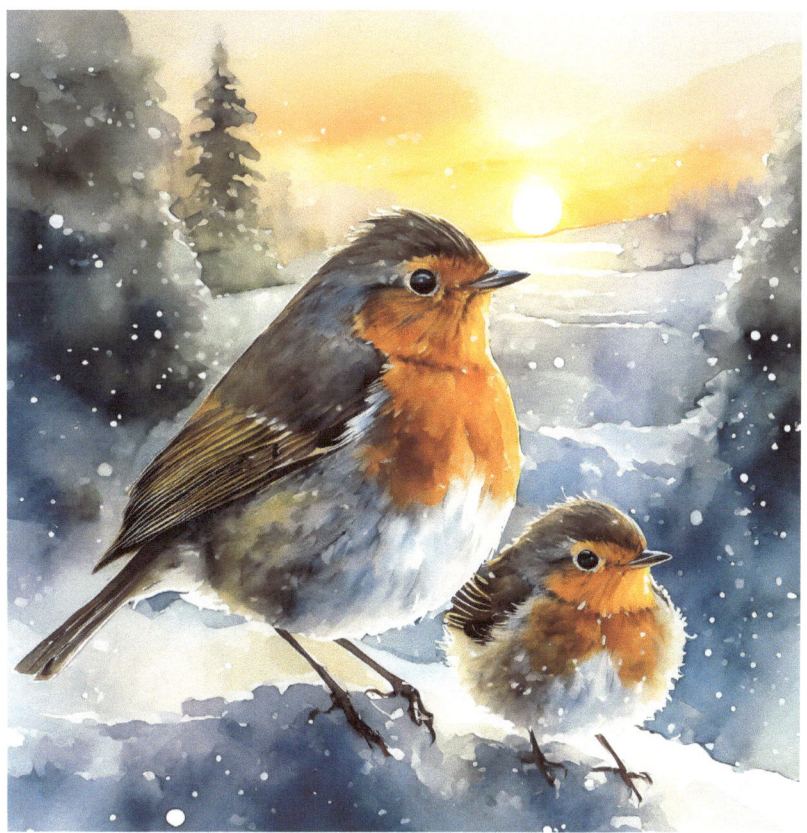

Chapter 8

Threats and Conservation

Raising Awareness About Threats to Bird Populations:

Birds, with their vibrant colors, melodious songs, and remarkable behaviors, enrich our lives and ecosystems in countless ways. However, these beloved avian creatures face a myriad of threats that jeopardize their survival and well-being. In this chapter, we shed light on the pressing issues confronting bird populations worldwide, including habitat loss, climate change, pollution, and human disturbance.

Habitat Loss and Degradation:

One of the greatest threats to bird populations is habitat loss and degradation, driven primarily by human activities such as deforestation, urbanization, agriculture, and infrastructure development. As natural habitats are converted into farmland, cities, and industrial zones, birds lose vital nesting sites, foraging grounds, and stopover sites crucial for migration. Fragmentation of habitat further isolates bird populations, leading to decreased genetic diversity and increased vulnerability to predation and disease.

Climate Change:

Climate change poses a significant threat to bird populations, altering temperature patterns, precipitation levels, and habitat distributions around the world. Rising temperatures can disrupt breeding cycles, shift migratory patterns, and reduce food availability for birds, leading to population declines and range contractions. Extreme weather events such as hurricanes, droughts, and heatwaves can also devastate bird habitats and populations, exacerbating the challenges they face in a changing climate.

Pollution:

Pollution, in various forms such as air pollution, water pollution, and noise pollution, poses significant risks to bird populations and ecosystems. Pesticides and chemical pollutants can accumulate in bird tissues, causing reproductive abnormalities, immune system suppression, and population declines. Plastic pollution, ingestion of microplastics, and oil spills can also have lethal consequences for birds, leading to entanglement, suffocation, and poisoning.

Human Disturbance:

Human disturbance, including habitat destruction, noise pollution, hunting, and tourism, can disrupt bird behaviors, breeding activities, and foraging patterns. Nest disturbance during the breeding season can cause nest abandonment, decreased reproductive success, and population declines. Recreational activities such as birdwatching, photography, and wildlife tourism, when not conducted responsibly, can also disturb birds and their habitats, leading to stress and habitat degradation.

Highlighting Conservation Efforts and Success Stories:

Despite the formidable challenges facing bird populations, there is hope for their conservation and recovery. Conservation organizations, governments, scientists, and local communities around the world are working tirelessly to protect bird habitats, implement sustainable land-use practices, and mitigate the impacts of threats such as habitat loss, climate change, and pollution.

Success stories abound, showcasing the power of conservation efforts to make a positive difference for birds and their ecosystems. Habitat restoration projects, protected area designations, and community-based conservation initiatives have led to the recovery of threatened bird species, the restoration of degraded habitats, and the establishment of conservation corridors to connect fragmented landscapes.

International collaborations, such as migratory bird treaties and global conservation agreements, have also played a crucial role in protecting migratory bird populations and their habitats across international borders. Citizen science initiatives, involving birdwatchers and volunteers in data collection and monitoring efforts, have provided valuable insights into bird populations, distributions, and behaviors, informing conservation strategies and management decisions.

Conclusion:

As we conclude our exploration of the threats faced by bird populations and the conservation efforts underway to protect them, let us recognize the urgent need for action to safeguard the future of birds and their ecosystems. By raising awareness, supporting conservation initiatives, and advocating for policy changes, we can make a meaningful difference in preserving the rich diversity of bird life on our planet for generations to come. Together, we can ensure that birds continue to inspire, delight, and enrich our lives and ecosystems for centuries to come.

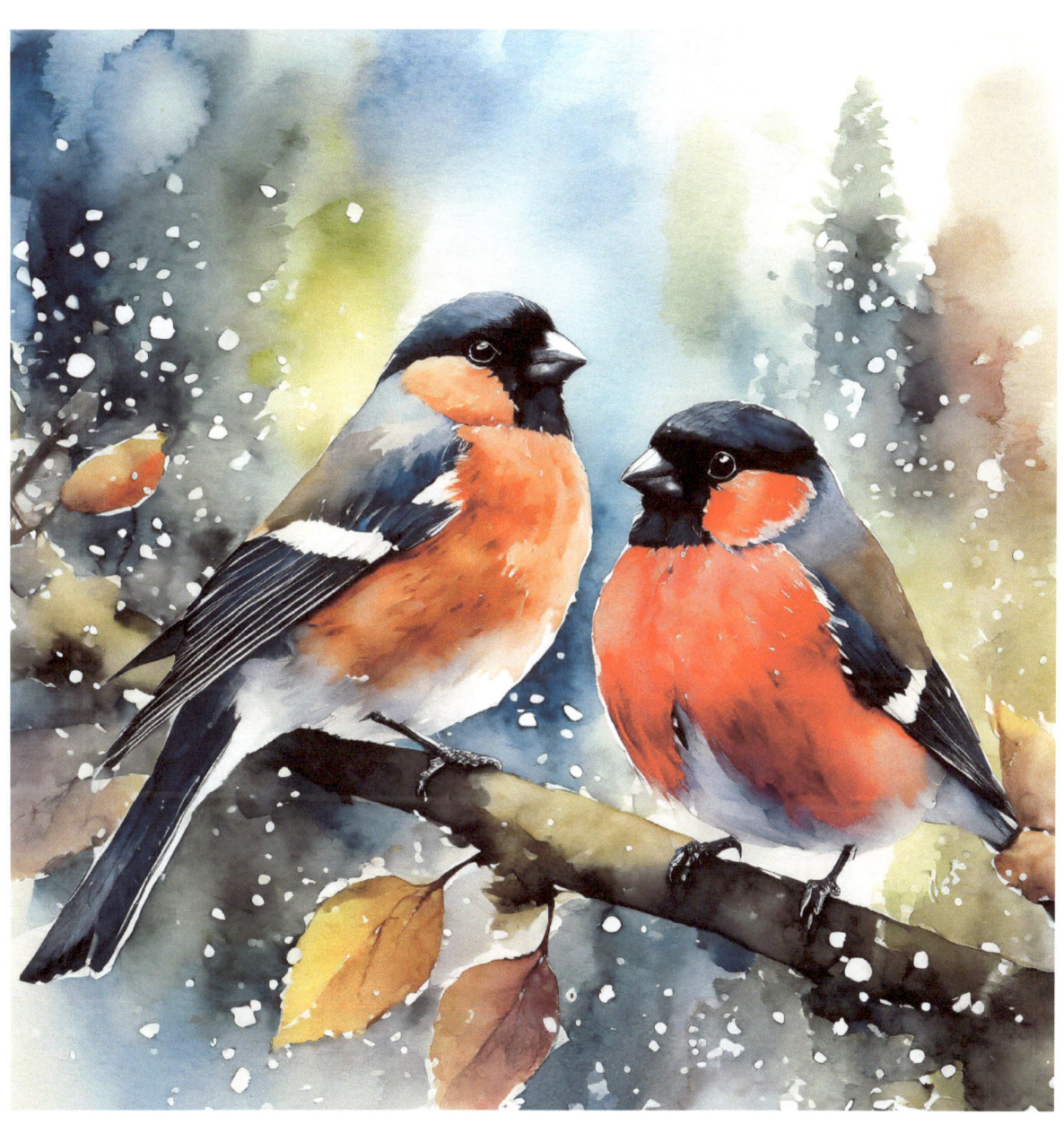

Chapter 9

Birds in Culture and Mythology

Exploring the Significance of Birds in Human Culture:

Birds have played a central role in human culture, art, and mythology for millennia, captivating our imagination with their beauty, grace, and mystique. From ancient civilizations to modern societies, birds have inspired awe, wonder, and reverence, shaping our cultural beliefs, artistic expressions, and spiritual practices.

In this chapter, we delve into the rich tapestry of human-bird interactions, exploring the diverse ways in which birds have influenced storytelling, symbolism, and spiritual beliefs across cultures and continents.

Birds as Symbols of Freedom and Flight:

Throughout history, birds have been revered as symbols of freedom, flight, and transcendence, representing the human desire to break free from earthly constraints and soar to new heights of possibility. In myths and legends, birds are often depicted as messengers of the gods, carrying divine messages between the heavens and the earth. The image of birds in flight has inspired artists, poets, and philosophers, symbolizing the pursuit of knowledge, enlightenment, and spiritual liberation.

Birds in Mythology and Folklore:

In cultures around the world, birds feature prominently in myths, legends, and folklore, embodying a wide range of symbolic meanings and archetypal roles. In ancient Egypt, the ibis was associated with the god Thoth, the patron of wisdom and writing, while the phoenix symbolized death and rebirth in Greek mythology. In Native American traditions, the eagle is revered as a symbol of strength, courage, and vision, while the raven is seen as a trickster and creator figure in many indigenous cultures.

Birds in Art and Literature:

Birds have long been a source of inspiration for artists, writers, and poets, who have captured their beauty, grace, and majesty in paintings, sculptures, and literary works. From the intricate bird mosaics of ancient Rome to the delicate bird motifs of traditional Japanese art, birds have been celebrated as symbols of grace, beauty, and harmony in visual arts. In literature, birds have been featured in countless stories, poems, and fables, serving as metaphors for human emotions, desires, and aspirations.

Birds in Spiritual Beliefs and Practices:

Birds have held sacred significance in many spiritual traditions and belief systems, symbolizing divine guidance, protection, and transformation. In Hindu mythology, the peacock is associated with the goddess Saraswati, the patron of knowledge and wisdom, while the owl is revered as a symbol of wisdom and foresight in Native American cultures. In Christianity, the dove is a symbol of the Holy Spirit and peace, representing the presence of God in the world.

Conclusion:

As we conclude our exploration of birds in culture and mythology, let us reflect on the profound impact these magnificent creatures have had on human societies throughout history. From their symbolism in religious rituals and artistic expressions to their roles in storytelling and spiritual beliefs, birds continue to inspire, intrigue, and enrich our lives in countless ways. By honoring and preserving the cultural heritage of birds, we pay tribute to the enduring bond between humans and the natural world, fostering a deeper appreciation for the beauty, diversity, and wonder of avian life on our planet.

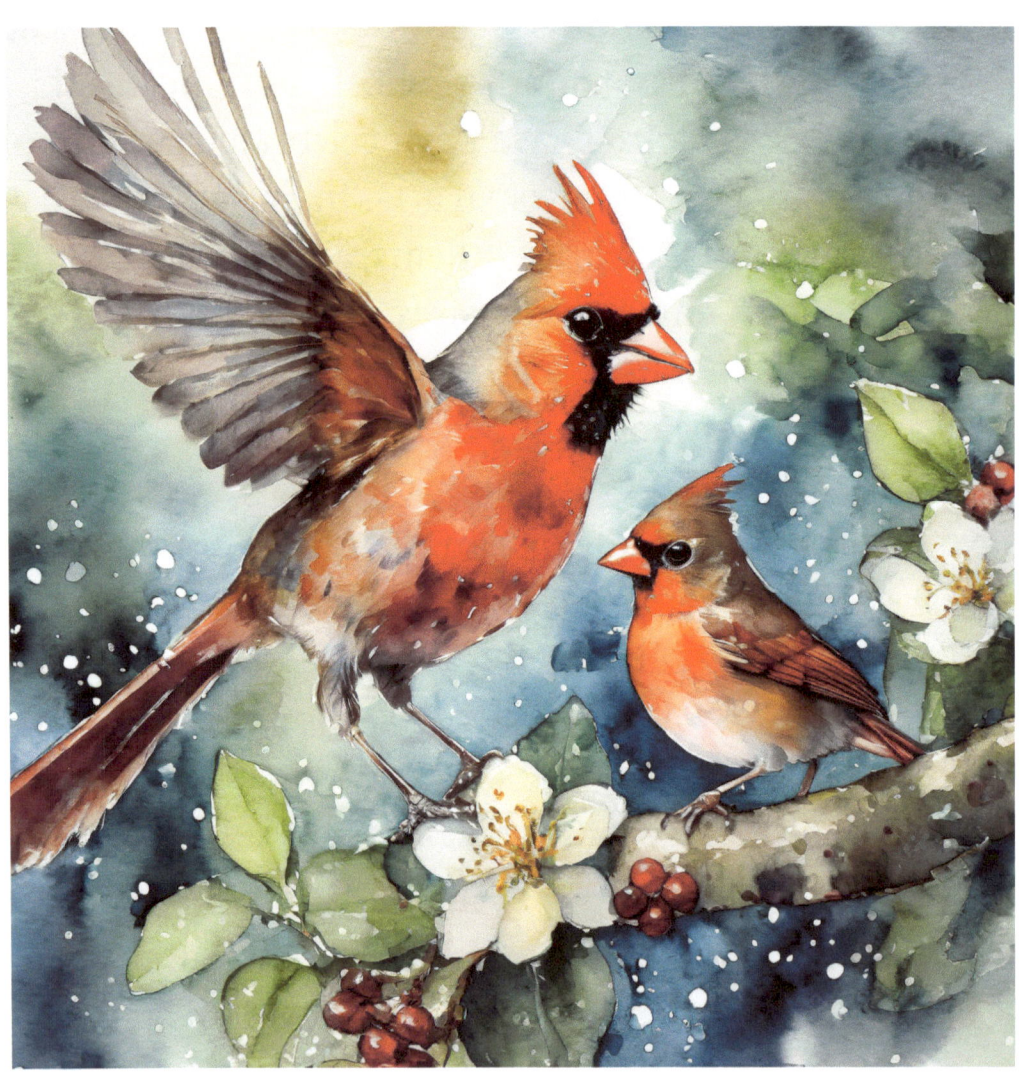

Chapter 10

The Future of Avian Life

Importance of Protecting Bird Habitats and Biodiversity:

As we stand at the threshold of a new era, the future of avian life hangs in the balance, facing unprecedented challenges and uncertainties. In this final chapter, we reflect on the importance of safeguarding bird habitats and biodiversity for future generations, recognizing the integral role birds play in maintaining healthy ecosystems and sustaining life on our planet.

Preserving Ecosystem Services:

Birds are vital components of ecosystems, serving as pollinators, seed dispersers, pest controllers, and indicators of environmental health. By protecting bird habitats and biodiversity, we not only preserve the ecological balance of natural systems but also safeguard essential ecosystem services that support human well-being, such as clean air, clean water, and fertile soils. Healthy bird populations contribute to the resilience of ecosystems, helping to mitigate the impacts of climate change, habitat loss, and pollution.

Conserving Cultural Heritage:

Birds are not only ecological treasures but also cultural icons, deeply ingrained in the traditions, beliefs, and identities of human societies around the world. By protecting bird habitats and biodiversity, we preserve the cultural heritage of birds and the rich tapestry of stories, myths, and legends they inspire.

From indigenous ceremonies and spiritual practices to artistic expressions and literary works, birds continue to shape our cultural landscapes and connect us to the wonders of the natural world.

Promoting Sustainable Development:

Sustainable development is essential for achieving a harmonious balance between human needs and the conservation of natural resources. By integrating bird conservation into land-use planning, resource management, and policy decision-making, we can promote sustainable development practices that support both human livelihoods and biodiversity conservation. From implementing protected areas and wildlife corridors to promoting eco-tourism and sustainable agriculture, there are many ways to reconcile human development with the needs of birds and other wildlife.

Ways to Get Involved in Bird Conservation Efforts:

There are countless ways for individuals, communities, and organizations to get involved in bird conservation efforts and make a positive impact on the future of avian life. Here are some actionable steps readers can take to support bird conservation:

Support Conservation Organizations: Donate to reputable bird conservation organizations and participate in volunteer programs, citizen science projects, and advocacy campaigns aimed at protecting bird habitats and biodiversity.

Create Bird-Friendly Habitats: Plant native trees, shrubs, and flowers in your garden or community spaces to provide food, shelter, and nesting sites for birds. Reduce pesticide use and minimize light pollution to create safer environments for birds to thrive.

Promote Sustainable Practices: Advocate for sustainable land-use practices, renewable energy solutions, and wildlife-friendly policies at the local, national, and international levels. Encourage businesses and governments to prioritize conservation and sustainability in their decision-making processes.

Educate and Raise Awareness: Share information about the importance of bird conservation with your family, friends, and community members. Organize educational events, workshops, and outreach activities to raise awareness about the threats facing birds and inspire collective action for their protection.

Celebrate Birds: Participate in birdwatching, bird photography, and bird-related events to celebrate the beauty, diversity, and wonder of avian life. Join bird clubs, birding festivals, and birding tours to connect with fellow bird enthusiasts and learn more about birds in your local area and beyond.

Conclusion:

As we look to the future of avian life, let us embrace the challenge and opportunity to protect and preserve the natural world for generations to come. By recognizing the importance of bird habitats and biodiversity, promoting sustainable development practices, and actively engaging in bird conservation efforts, we can ensure a brighter future for birds and humanity alike.

Conclusion:

As we conclude our journey through the captivating world of avian life, we are left in awe of the wonder and beauty that birds bring to our planet. From the majestic eagles soaring high above the mountains to the delicate hummingbirds flitting among tropical flowers, birds enrich our lives in countless ways, reminding us of the boundless creativity and diversity of the natural world.

Birds are more than just creatures of flight; they are integral components of ecosystems, playing vital roles as pollinators, seed dispersers, and indicators of environmental health. Their presence is a testament to the interconnectedness of all living things and the delicate balance that sustains life on Earth.

As stewards of our planet, it is our responsibility to cherish and protect the world of avian life for future generations. By continuing to explore, appreciate, and learn about birds, we deepen our connection to the natural world and cultivate a sense of reverence and respect for all living beings.

Let us heed the call to action and commit ourselves to the conservation of bird habitats and biodiversity. Through collective efforts and individual actions, we can make a meaningful difference in preserving the beauty and wonder of avian life for generations to come.

So, let us spread our wings and soar into the future with hope and determination, guided by the enduring spirit of birds and the promise of a world where nature thrives in harmony with humanity. Together, let us ensure that the skies remain filled with the song and flight of birds, inspiring wonder and awe in all who behold them.

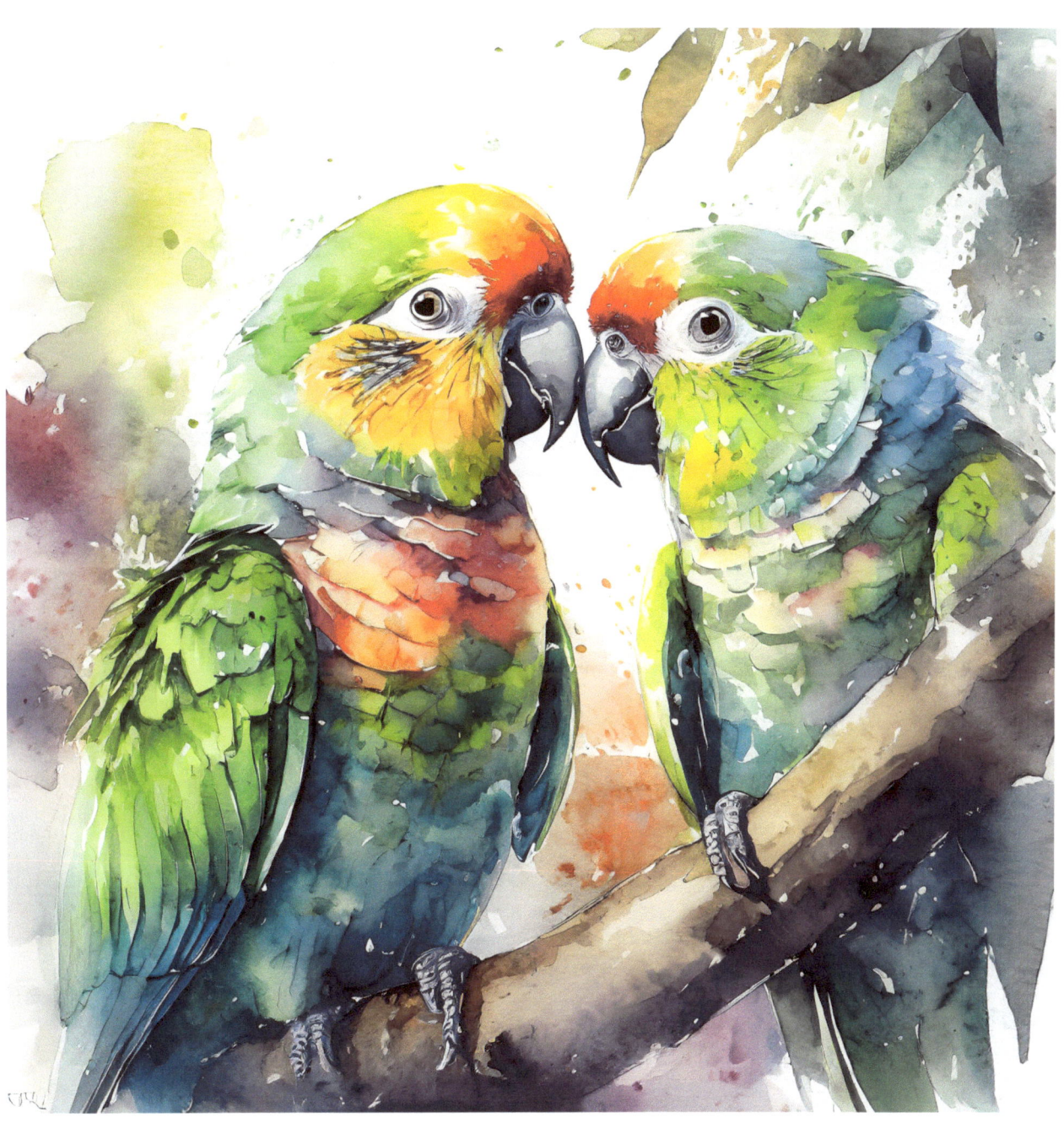

In my next book I will incorporate specific bird species, their habitats, behaviours, and unique characteristics to captivate my readers.

Title: "Wings of Enchantment: A Journey Through the Lives of Extraordinary Birds"

Introduction:

Welcome to "Wings of Enchantment," where we embark on a captivating journey through the lives of extraordinary birds. In this book, we delve deep into the fascinating world of avian diversity, exploring the habitats, behaviors, and unique characteristics of some of the most captivating bird species on the planet.

Chapter 1: The Enigmatic Hummingbird

Discover the enchanting world of hummingbirds, known for their iridescent plumage, hovering flight, and rapid wingbeats. Explore their specialized diets, intricate courtship displays, and remarkable migration journeys as they navigate diverse habitats from lush tropical forests to arid deserts.

Chapter 2: The Majestic Bald Eagle

Soar with the majestic bald eagle, an iconic symbol of strength and freedom. Learn about their impressive hunting prowess, intricate nesting behaviors, and the challenges they face in their efforts to thrive in habitats ranging from pristine wilderness to urban landscapes.

Chapter 3: The Whimsical Penguin

Dive into the icy waters of the Southern Hemisphere to encounter the whimsical world of penguins. Witness their playful antics on land and their graceful underwater ballet as they navigate the challenges of life in some of the harshest environments on Earth.

Chapter 4: The Regal Peacock

Marvel at the regal beauty of the peacock, with its resplendent plumage and mesmerizing courtship displays. Explore the cultural significance of this iconic bird in mythology, art, and literature, and discover its unique adaptations for survival in diverse habitats.

Chapter 5: The Mystical Owl

Enter the realm of mystery and magic with the mystical owl, revered for its nocturnal wisdom and silent flight. Learn about their extraordinary hunting techniques, intricate vocalizations, and symbolic significance in cultures around the world.

Chapter 6: The Graceful Crane

Witness the elegant grace of cranes as they dance across wetlands and soar through the skies in synchronized flight. Explore their complex social behaviors, elaborate courtship rituals, and the vital role they play in maintaining healthy ecosystems.

Chapter 7: The Vibrant Toucan

Journey to the colorful rainforests of Central and South America to encounter the vibrant toucan. Admire their striking beaks, melodic calls, and unique feeding behaviors, and discover how they contribute to the rich biodiversity of their tropical habitats.

Chapter 8: The Resilient Albatross

Sail the open seas with the resilient albatross, masters of long-distance flight and skilled navigators of the world's oceans. Learn about their epic migration journeys, intricate mating rituals, and the conservation challenges they face in a changing world.

Conclusion:

As we conclude our journey through the lives of extraordinary birds, may we continue to be inspired by their beauty, resilience, and grace. Let us cherish and protect these magnificent creatures and the habitats they depend on, ensuring a bright and sustainable future for birds and humans alike.

OpenAI. (2024). ChatGPT (3.5) [Large language model]. https://chat.openai.com

Appendix

Glossary of Birding Terms:

Binoculars: Optical instruments used for magnifying distant objects, essential for birdwatching.

Field Guide: A book containing illustrations or photographs of birds, along with information on their identification, behavior, and habitat.

Migration: The seasonal movement of birds between breeding and wintering grounds, often spanning vast distances.
Endemic: Species that are native and restricted to a particular geographic region.

Pelagic: Referring to birds that spend most of their lives at sea, away from land.

Raptor: Birds of prey, including eagles, hawks, falcons, and owls, known for their hunting prowess.

Plumage: The feathers covering a bird's body, often colorful and distinctive in appearance.

Molt: The process of shedding old feathers and replacing them with new ones, typically occurring once or twice a year.

Vagrant: A bird that is outside its normal range or expected habitat, often due to migration errors or extreme weather events.

Songbird: Passerine birds known for their melodious vocalizations, including warblers, thrushes, and sparrows.

Recommended Resources for Further Reading:

Field Guides:

"The Sibley Guide to Birds" by David Allen Sibley
"National Geographic Field Guide to the Birds of North America" by Jon L. Dunn and Jonathan Alderfer
"The Birds of Europe" by Lars Svensson, Killian Mullarney, and Dan Zetterström

Books on Bird Behavior and Ecology:

"The Genius of Birds" by Jennifer Ackerman
"Bird Sense: What It's Like to Be a Bird" by Tim Birkhead
"The Homing Instinct: Meaning and Mystery in Animal Migration" by Bernd Heinrich
Birdwatching Magazines and Journals:

"Birdwatching Magazine"
"Audubon Magazine"
"The Auk: Ornithological Advances"

Online Resources:

Cornell Lab of Ornithology: https://www.birds.cornell.edu/
eBird: https://ebird.org/home

BirdLife International: https://www.birdlife.org/

Podcasts:

"BirdNote" - A podcast featuring short stories about birds and the environment.
"Out There with the Birds" - A podcast covering various aspects of birdwatching, birding travel, and conservation.

List of Birdwatching Organizations:

Audubon Society: A nonprofit organization dedicated to bird conservation and habitat protection.

BirdLife International: A global partnership of conservation organizations working to conserve birds and their habitats.

National Audubon Society: A grassroots conservation organization focused on protecting birds and their habitats in North America.

Royal Society for the Protection of Birds (RSPB): A UK-based charity dedicated to bird conservation and wildlife protection.

American Birding Association (ABA): An organization focused on promoting birdwatching and bird conservation through education, publications, and advocacy.

These organizations offer opportunities for birdwatchers to connect with like-minded individuals, participate in conservation initiatives, and contribute to our understanding and appreciation of birds and their habitats.

To the Reader,

In closing, may the beauty and wonder of the avian world continue to inspire and uplift us. Let us carry forward the lessons learned from these extraordinary birds, cherishing their habitats and striving to ensure their survival for generations to come. Thank you for joining me on this journey through the skies. Until we meet again, may your spirit soar with the wings of enchantment.

With heartfelt gratitude,

Shazia Naqib